BIBLE 12
CHRISTIAN MIN.

CONTENTS

I. DEFINING MINISTRY **2**

BIBLICAL VARIETIES **2**

THE TWO MODERN MEANINGS **4**

II. MINISTRY OCCUPATIONS **9**

CHURCHES **9**

MISSIONARY ORGANIZATIONS **10**

MOVEMENTS **12**

SCHOOLS **13**

SOCIAL SERVICES **14**

MEDIA COMMUNICATIONS **15**

SUPPORT SERVICES **16**

III. MINISTRY VS. CAREER **20**

WHEN THEY ARE THE SAME **21**

WHEN THEY ARE SEPARATE **22**

GLOSSARY **26**

Author: **Barry G. Burrus, M.Div, M.A., B.S.**

Editor: Alan Christopherson, M.S.

Illustrations: Roberta Sinnock

                 Kyle R. Bennett, A.S.

Alpha Omega Publications ®

804 North 2nd Avenue East, Rock Rapids, Iowa 51246-1759

BIBLE 1202
CHRISTIAN MINISTRIES

CONTENTS

I. DRESSING MINISTRY 2

    BIBLICAL VARIETIES 2

    THE TWO MODERN MEANINGS 4

II. MINISTRY OCCUPATIONS 8

    CHURCHES 9

    MISSIONARY ORGANIZATIONS 10

    MOVEMENTS 12

    SCHOOLS 13

    SOCIAL SERVICES 14

    MEDIA COMMUNICATIONS 15

    SUPPORT SERVICES 16

III. MINISTRY VS. CAREER 20

    WHEN THEY ARE THE SAME 21

    WHEN THEY ARE SEPARATE 22

GLOSSARY 25

Author: Barry Oesterlin, MEd, MA, BS

Editor: Alan Christopherson, MS

Illustrator: Dom Robertson

Kyle R. Bennett, A.S.

Alpha Omega Publications®

804 N. 2nd Ave. E., Rock Rapids, IA 51246-1759
© MM by Alpha Omega Publications, Inc. All rights reserved.
LIFEPAC is a registered trademark of Alpha Omega Publications, Inc.

CHRISTIAN MINISTRIES

Career guidance begins with self-understanding, but the next step is equally essential: knowing the job market. Then you can intelligently match yourself with a suitable career.

Information about secular occupations is more readily available than information about ministries. *The Dictionary of Occupational Titles*, published by the United States Department of Labor, describes almost twenty nine thousand occupational titles. Of all these occupations, only eight are related to religion, theology, and churches. The emphasis of this LIFEPAC® is upon the variety of Christian ministry.

OBJECTIVES

Read these objectives. The objectives tell you what you will be able to do when you have successfully completed this LIFEPAC.

When you have finished this LIFEPAC, you should be able to:

1. Explain what a Christian ministry is.
2. Describe the various kinds of Christian ministries.
3. Compare a Christian ministry to a career.

Survey the LIFEPAC. Ask yourself some questions about this study. Write your questions here.

_____

_____

_____

_____

_____

_____

_____

_____

I. DEFINING MINISTRY

A lively discussion occupied Mr. Newman's classroom. "What is a Christian ministry?" he asked. Craig volunteered an answer, "Something you do for God." Immediately Edith replied, "But ministry also is helping people." "Isn't it what you do in church?" asked Helen. Jordan thought aloud about pastors and missionaries being ministers. "But anyone who uses the Bible is ministering," added Dan. "Any spiritual work," concluded Ruth, "is ministering."

Which answers from the class do you think were correct? A survey of Christian ministries reveals that they encompass all of these and more. Christian ministries are performed in a multitude of ways both in the Bible and in Christendom.

This section examines the varieties of ministries in the New Testament and interprets the meaning of ministry for Christians today.

SECTION OBJECTIVES

Review these objectives. When you have completed this section, you should be able to:

1. Name and define two classifications of New Testament ministries.
2. Give the New Testament meaning of the word ministry.
3. Define ministry as viewed in Christendom today.
4. Correct five misconceptions related to persons in and functions of ministries.

 Read Romans 15:8,15-16,25-27,30-31; 16:1-6 and 12.

 From the preceding verses, list in your *career notebook* the names of those who minister or serve in any way, and then describe how (Assignment 10).

BIBLICAL VARIETIES

In the Greek language (the original language of the New Testament), the main word for minister or servant is *deacon* (1 Timothy 3:13). A different word, however, is used for slaves (bond servants). Thus, *ministry* in the New Testament means *voluntary service for other persons.*

First Corinthians 12:5 declares, "And there are differences of administrations [varieties of ministries]..." Accordingly, many different kinds of ministries are performed in the New Testament. They may be classified as either general services or special ministries.

General Services. In the New Testament, general services appear in the form of *assistance* rendered mainly for the benefit of fellow believers, performed by serving meals, supplying money or goods, and caring for physical needs. Examples of these three kinds of services are given:

Serving meals. Martha, the sister of Mary, is remembered for receiving a rebuke by Jesus (Luke 10:38-42); but in John 12:2 she served Jesus a meal again, but without rebuke.

Money or goods. The church in Antioch ministered to the material needs of its mother church (Acts 11:27-30). When a prophet foretold a famine in Jerusalem, they decided to send the church in Jerusalem *relief.* The word, translated *relief* (verse 29), is the main word used for ministry in the Greek New Testament.

Caring for physical needs. While Paul was in a Roman prison, Christians stayed by his side to render him personal aid. One of these Christians was a runaway slave named Onesimus. Paul had led him to faith in Christ and then sent him back to his Christian master, Philemon. Paul wrote that he wished he could keep Onesimus to be his own servant (Philemon 13).

Special Ministries. Special ministries in the New Testament are duties performed primarily to propagate the Gospel and maintain the unity of the Church. Jesus said (John 12:26), "If any man serve me, let him follow me..." Although every spiritual gift equips for ministry, one gift itself is actually named *ministry* (Romans 12:7). Generally, special ministries appear in the New Testament in association with certain individuals and groups:

1. Individuals who perform special ministries in the New Testament include both men and women, the prominent and obscure.
2. Groups or classes of people who perform special ministries in the New Testament include both leaders and lay members of the church. The New Testament cites the ministries of the Old Testament priests (Hebrews 10:11) and prophets (1 Peter 1:12). The most prominent ministries in the New Testament were those of the apostles (Acts 1:25). Deacons by definition are ministers (1 Timothy 3:13). The ministry of the church is

PERFORMING A BIBLICAL SPECIAL MINISTRY

also performed by all of the saints (Ephesians 4:12).

This overview of *ministry* in the New Testament forms our foundation for understanding what ministry is.

![pen icon] **Complete these activities.**

1.1 Read the following Bible verses and list the names of individuals in them who performed ministries:

a. Acts 12:25 (2 people) _____

b. Romans 15:8; 16:1 (2 people) _____

c. 1 Corinthians 3:5 (2 people) _____

d. Colossians 1:7; 4:7; and 4:17 (3 people) _____

e. 1 Thessalonians 3:2 (1 person) _____

1.2 The New Testament cites the ministries of the Old Testament as a. _____ and b. _____

1.3 The most prominent ministries in the New Testament were those of the _____ .

1.4 By definition, deacons are _____ .

1.5 The ministry of the church includes _____ saints.

![pen icon] **Match these items.**

1.6 _____ general service

1.7 _____ prepared a meal for Jesus

1.8 _____ ministered to the material needs of the church in Jerusalem

1.9 _____ rendered Paul personal aid

1.10 _____ special ministry

a. the church in Antioch

b. assistance to fellow believers

c. Philemon

d. propagate the Gospel

e. Martha

f. Onesimus

THE TWO MODERN MEANINGS

Ministry in the New Testament is synonymous with service. It performs general services for other people and it performs special ministries to maintain the unity of the church. As viewed in Christendom today, the word ministry conveys two distinct meanings, a *restrictive meaning* and an *inclusive meaning*.

Restrictive. The restrictive meaning of ministry identifies it purely as the Gospel ministry, under those such as pastors and missionaries. Ministry is frequently limited to this meaning.

Inclusive. The inclusive meaning of ministry includes the voluntary ministries performed by all Christians. Ministry in this sense corresponds more closely to the Biblical use of the word as it is used for a wide variety of Christian services. The following segments correct five misconceptions that arise from limiting the definition of a ministry.

1. Ministries are performed not only by the leaders of churches and Christian organizations but also by Christian followers. All the redeemed have a responsibility to the Lord's work.

2. Ministry is the duty of not only men but also of women. A Christian woman is just as responsible to serve the Lord as is a Christian man. In the Bible many women served their responsibility to the Lord. They were involved especially in such general services as household ministries and caring for people's physical needs (Luke 4:39 and 8:3), but were not exempt from special ministries. The late Henrietta Mears sponsored a ministry to college-aged youth in a large church. Her ministry to them inspired dozens of young people to give their lives to serve the Lord. In addition, Ms. Mears founded a Sunday school literature publishing company that became one of the largest Christian publishers.

3. Ministries include part-time and volunteer services as well as full-time vocations. For instance, you don't have to become a missionary to share Christ with non-christians. Ken Norem was a welder by trade, but he devoted certain evenings of the week to visiting homes in his community for the Church. Because of Ken's gospel

PEOPLE IN MINISTRIES

NOT ONLY　　　　　　　　　　　　　　　　　　**BUT ALSO**

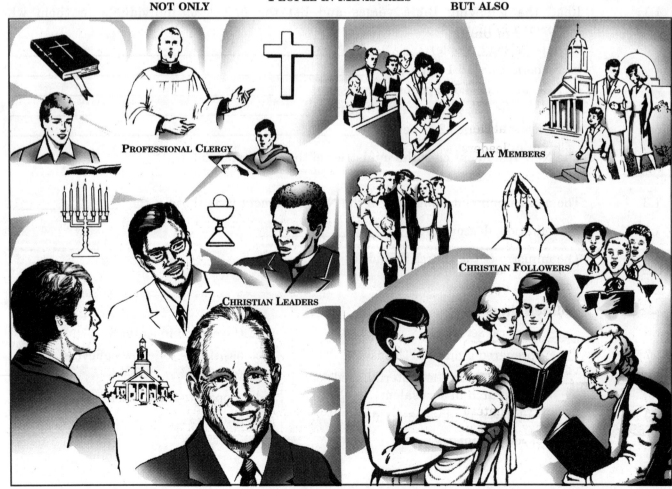

PROFESSIONAL CLERGY

LAY MEMBERS

CHRISTIAN LEADERS

CHRISTIAN FOLLOWERS

proclamations, many people repented and joined the Body of Christ.

4. Ministry is both church-related and community-centered activities. Some extra-church ministries are more significant than some church activities. For example, singing in a church choir is a relatively minor role, while directing a rescue mission on skid row is a major one.

5. A ministry need not be religious in nature. It may have an essentially secular nature and still be used as a channel of ministry. Missionary doctors heal bodies medically, and in turn have the opportunity to proclaim the Gospel. The work of a church custodian is essential for the efficient functioning of Sunday school classes. We minister to everyone through the example of our honorable lives and friendly attitudes.

Answer these questions.

1.11   What is the *restrictive* meaning of ministry (explain fully)? _____

_____

_____

_____

1.12   What is the *inclusive* meaning of ministry (explain fully)? _____

_____

_____

_____

Complete this chart.

not only...	but also...
Persons in Ministries	
1.13 Professional clergy	_____
1.14 Christian leaders	_____
1.15 Men	_____
Functions in Ministries	
1.16 Church-related	_____
1.17 Full-time vocations	_____
1.18 Of a religious nature	_____

Review the material in this section in preparation for the Self Test. This Self Test will check your mastery of this particular section. The items missed on this Self Test will indicate specific areas where restudy is needed for mastery.

NOT ONLY...

SACRAMENTS, VOCATIONS, THE SACRED

BUT ALSO...

VOLUNTEERS, COMMUNITY SERVICE, THE SECULAR

Match these items (each answer, 2 points).

1.01	_____ deacon	a. propagate the Gospel
1.02	_____ ministry	b. prepared Jesus a meal
1.03	_____ general service	c. is the main word for *minister* in Greek
1.04	_____ special ministry	d. ministered to the church at Antioch
1.05	_____ Onesimus	e. means *volunteer service for others*
1.06	_____ Barnabas and Saul (Paul)	f. a servant of the church in Thessalonica
1.07	_____ Martha	g. Onisemus' Christian master
1.08	_____ Restrictive	h. rendered Paul personal aid
1.09	_____ Inclusive	i. volunteers
1.010	_____ Philemon	j. rendered mainly for the benefit of fellow believers
		k. pastors and missionaries

Complete these statements (each answer, 3 points).

1.011 *Ministry* in the New Testament is synonymous with _____ .

1.012 For a Christian, then, *ministry* means _____ .

1.013 The three kinds of service are a. _____ , b. _____ , and
c. _____

1.014 Ministry is not only the duty of men, but also _____ .

1.015 In the Bible women were involved in such a. _____ services as
b. _____ ministries and caring for people's c. _____ needs.

1.016 A ministry _____ (does, does not) need to be sacred in nature.

Choose the correct answer (each numbered item, 2 points).

1.017 *The Dictionary of Occupational Titles*, published by the United States Department of Labor,
describes about _____ thousand occupational titles.
a. ten   b. twenty nine   c. forty five

1.018 Of all the occupations described in *The Dictionary of Occupational Titles*, only _____ are
related to religion, theology, and churches.
a. eight   b. five   c. one hundred

1.019 The main word used for *ministry* in the Greek New Testament is the word translated ____ in
Acts 11:29.
a. service   b. relief   c. deacon

1.020 A runaway slave whom Paul led to Christ and then sent back to his Christian master was ____ .
a. Onesimus   b. Tychicus   c. Philemon

1.021 The most prominent ministries in the New Testament were those of the _____ .
a. disciples   b. deacons   c. apostles

1.022 The ministries of the church include _____ .
a. pastors and deacons   b. pastors and missionaries   c. all saints

Complete this chart (each answer, 3 points).

	not only...	but also...
	Persons in Ministries	
1.023	Professional clergy	_____
1.024	Christian leaders	_____
1.025	Men	_____
	Functions in Ministries	
1.026	Church-related	_____
1.027	Full-time vocations	_____
1.028	Of a religious nature	_____

Answer these questions (each question, 5 points).

1.029   What is the New Testament definition of *ministry*? _____

_____

_____

1.030   Into what two classifications may the many different ministries performed in the New Testament be classified?

a. _____

b. _____

1.031   What is the meaning of this statement: "A ministry need not be sacred in nature"?

_____

_____

_____

Score _____

Adult check _____

            Initial   Date

II. MINISTRY OCCUPATIONS

How many occupations exist in the world today? One thousand? Ten thousand? The Dictionary of Occupational Titles describes about twenty nine thousand occupational titles in the United States. Estimates of the total number of occupations in the world range up to one hundred thousand, with new and different kinds of jobs being created all the time.

Christian ministries too, are surprisingly numerous and varied. The Sunday school board of one denomination employs about fifteen hundred persons alone with over four hundred different job titles. Openings in the "Christian job market" can be found for almost any skill, talent, gift or combination of these three. As a rule, larger churches, institutions, and organizations seek specialists who concentrate in a narrow field. Smaller churches seek generalists with abilities to perform more than one type of ministry.

This section describes over one hundred separate religious ministries. They are representative of the wide variety of ministries and services performed by Christians. Their number and variety expands constantly.

Churches today are developing more unconventional ministries than ever before, and church members are becoming more involved. Christian organizations are employing more workers in secular support services as ministries are springing up outside the church establishment.

This section identifies seven categories of Christian ministries: (1) Church-related ministries, (2) missionary organizations, (3) movements, (4) schools, (5) social services, (6) communications, and (7) personal support services. Positions that belong to more than one category are usually listed only once.

SECTION OBJECTIVES

Review these objectives. When you have completed this section, you should be able to:

1. Identify seven categories of Christian ministries.
2. Describe several religious ministries and related services.

CHURCHES

By a wide margin, church-related positions are the most plentiful and visible ministries. They are described in three levels: pastoral, office, and denominational staffs.

Pastoral Staffs. Pastoral staffs vary among churches in the number and positions of staff people. A survey indicated that four of every five churches serve two hundred people or less. Only one of every twenty churches serves over three hundred fifty people. Therefore, the majority of churches employ only a single pastor. The pastor who is alone in a church is required to preach, teach, study, administer the Sacraments, counsel, moderate meetings, visit in homes, call in hospitals, do office work, carry on business, perform weddings, participate in social functions, meet with committees, plan activities, and so on indefinitely. Some need to supplement their income from other sources. An associate or assistant pastor usually takes responsibility for one or more individual pastoral functions including visitations, evangelism, outreach, discipleship, and membership training.

A director (or minister) of Christian education guides the teaching staff and program of the church, including Sunday school, training groups, doctrine (catechism) classes, vacation Bible school, and others. Some of the church staff may specialize in certain age groups such as youth and children's directors. Most churches obtain a music director either on an employed or volunteer basis, who makes arrangements for songleading, choir direction, and necessary materials. Recreational responsibilities, along with others, may also be delegated to a staff member. Small churches usually combine many of these duties for only one person.

Office Staffs. Office staffs in small churches usually begin with a part-time secretary. As the need for more help increases, churches add office helpers and then private secretaries for pastors. Secretaries often serve as receptionists, editors of church publications, and typists. They perform other clerical tasks such as mailing, filing, and copying. Large offices add bookkeepers and business administrators. An administrator supervises the various staffs, manages the church's finances, and properties.

Denominational Staffs. Denominational staffs are recruited from among church leaders who have proven themselves over time with a measure of excellence. Some are administrators; others are consultants. They specialize in missions, education, evangelism, campus ministry, finance, publications, communications, social service, research, public relations, church planting, construction, etc.

Complete this activity.

2.1 Underline the following *church-related ministries* that appeal to you. Then number those you have underlined in the order of their appeal to you, beginning with one for the most appealing.

____ pastor	____ church secretary
____ visitation pastor	____ office helper
____ evangelism	____ private secretary
____ discipleship	____ bookkeeper
____ education	____ business administrator
____ youth director	____ denominational administrator
____ children's director	____ denominational consultant
____ music director	____ traveling evangelist
____ recreation director	____ revivalist
____ traveling Bible teacher	____ other: _____
____ traveling discipler	____ _____

Complete these statements.

2.2 Church-related ministries are described in three levels: a. _____ ,
b. _____ , and c. _____ .

2.3 A survey indicated that four of every five churches serve _____ people or less.

2.4 Only one of every twenty churches serves over _____ people.

Match these items.

2.5 ____ proven excellence   a. pastoral staff

2.6 ____ church planting   b. office staff

2.7 ____ director of Christian education   c. denominational staff

2.8 ____ editor of church publication

2.9 ____ children's director

2.10 ____ business administrator

MISSIONARY ORGANIZATIONS

Missionaries perform most of the ministries described in the other categories. The principal difference is location. Home missionaries serve among special groups locally, whereas foreign missionaries serve in other countries.

Home Missions. Home missions in a broad sense include any organized ministry in the United States that is not self-supporting. Three types of home missions are church planting, ministries to ethnic groups, and the chaplaincy.

Church planting usually begins with a home missionary. The missionary surveys a residential community and generates interest in forming a new church. Then he conducts church services in temporary quarters until the group can obtain its own building. Meanwhile, he seeks additional people to join the growing group. He may be sponsored by a denomination, another church or individual contributors. Sometimes, he partially supports himself.

Certain *ethnic groups* in our country are the objects of home mission endeavors. Missionaries to Native Americans and Inuit (Eskimos) serve much as missionaries to other countries. Migrant farm workers and Jewish people are also sought as converts to Christ.

Chaplaincy ministries are provided mainly for the military forces, hospitals, and correctional institutions. Military chaplains function much as pastors do. They must be sponsored by a specific denomination or church group, and are required to attend seminary. Chaplains must excel in personal skills, for they often do much counseling in times of crisis. They are also commissioned officers of the United States military and subject to the UCMJ as well as God's laws.

Foreign missions. Foreign missions utilize the most varied ministries and services of any category. Nearly every ministry and service performed in the homeland is used on the mission field. Evangelists proclaim the Gospel, teachers educate the converts, and church staffs organize them into local groups. Most missions today emphasize church planting. In addition, they aim to train nationals to staff their own churches and to carry out the ministry on their own.

Missionary linguists seek to bridge language gaps. Translators put languages into written forms and translate the Bible into those languages so that nationals will be able to read the Bible in their own dialects.

Medical missionaries bring modern medicine to needy areas; and a few Christian physicians operate clinics or hospitals where nurses are always in demand. Dentists, pharmacists, and laboratory technicians also serve; sometimes only one person fills all of these roles. Agricultural missionaries help primitive people learn to feed themselves more adequately. Houseparents care for many missionary children in boarding schools.

Complete this activity.

2.11   Underline the following *missionary ministries* that appeal to you. Then number those you have underlined in the order of their appeal to you, beginning with one for the most appealing.

____ church planter   ____ evangelist

____ to native Americans   ____ teacher

____ to migrants   ____ pastor

____ to Jews   ____ linguist/translator

____ military   ____ doctor

____ hospital   ____ nurse

____ prison   ____ dentist

____ agricultural   ____ social worker

____ houseparent   ____ other: _____

Answer *true* **or** *false*.

2.12   _____   Missionaries perform few of the ministries described in the other categories of ministries.

2.13   _____   The principal difference between missions and other ministries is the location of service.

2.14   _____   Home missionaries serve among special local groups.

2.15   _____   Foreign missionaries serve in other countries.

2.16   _____   Church planting is limited to home missionaries.

2.17   _____   Foreign missions utilize the most varied ministries and services of any category of Christian ministries.

2.18   _____   Home missions are conducted mainly among migrant farm workers.

2.19   _____   Home missionaries to Jewish people seek to convert them to Christ.

| 2.20 | _____ | Chaplaincy ministries are provided for the military forces alone. |
| 2.21 | _____ | Caring for missionary children in a boarding school as houseparents can be a foreign-mission ministry. |

MOVEMENTS

A multitude of ministries have sprung up in response to special needs of particular classes of people. For example, many ministries to children utilize child evangelism methods. They form neighborhood Bible clubs or operate summer camping activities to teach children.

The most extensive programs developed during the past few decades minister to youth. Most youth ministries emphasize evangelism and discipleship. They do personal work, sponsor meetings, and provide fellowship activities such as concerts. Many student ministries operate on campuses, while some denominations establish student centers on or near campuses. One large Christian campus ministry employs five thousand staff members who raise their own support just as missionaries do. Also, coffee houses attempt to attract street people and to convert them to Christ.

Servicemen's centers (USO) placed in strategic locations seek to reach military personnel on leave. Rescue missions on skid row reach down-and-out transients and alcoholics who congregate in the inner cities. Such missions often provide food and overnight lodging with a Gospel proclamation. They strive to rehabilitate their converts and establish them in the faith.

Christian conference centers are popular with all ages, especially during the summertime. Many centers employ counseling staffs for children and youth camps as well as providing special speakers for the adults.

Ministries to families are multiplying. Many of these ministries conduct seminars in either specific churches or cities, offering self-improvement advice for marriage, parents, and family life. Fellowship organizations gather in local chapters for ministering to businessmen, women, single adults, and other special interest groups.

Complete this activity.

2.22   Underline the following *Christian movement ministries* that appeal to you. Then number those you have underlined in the order of their appeal to you, beginning with one for the most appealing.

___ children		___ music
___ teens		___ camp director
___ collegiate		___ camp counselor
___ service members		___ family seminar
___ rescue missions		___ Christian living seminar
___ women		___ businessmen
___ singles		___ other: _____

Choose the correct answer.

2.23   The most extensive programs among christian movements during the past few decades minister to _____ .

   a. children   c. adults

   b. youth   d. minorities

2.24   Coffee houses attempt to attract _____ people and to convert them to Christ.

   a. young   c. street

   b. service   d. married

2.25   Servicemen's centers are located strategically to reach military personnel _____ .

   a. on base   c. on duty

   b. on leave   d. A.W.O.L.

BIBLE

1 2 0 2

LIFEPAC TEST

56 / 70

Name _____

Date _____

Score _____

BIBLE 1202: LIFEPAC TEST

Answer *true* or *false* (each answer, 1 point).

1. _____ A Christian can have a ministry in a secular occupation.
2. _____ A series of similar jobs may be considered a vocation.
3. _____ One takes up an occupation to establish a way of living.
4. _____ One should take time from their secular work to witness.
5. _____ One's ministry off the job is served voluntarily.
6. _____ *Ministry* in the New Testament is synonymous with *service*.
7. _____ The special ministry propagates the Gospel.
8. _____ A ministry must be religious in nature.
9. _____ Pastors of smaller churches are likely to have more functions than pastors of larger churches.
10. _____ Members of church denominational staffs are usually chosen for a particular ministry because they excel in that ministry.

Complete these items (each answer, 3 points).

11. Two classifications of New Testament ministries are a. _____ services and b. ministries.

12. The category of Christian ministries that utilizes the most varied ministries is _____ .

13. One's ministry off the job is served _____ .

14. Every Christian is a _____ .

Match these items (each answer, 2 points).

15. _____ ministry
16. _____ general service
17. _____ special ministry
18. _____ restrictive meaning
19. _____ inclusive meaning
20. _____ office staff
21. _____ church planting
22. _____ Christian schools
23. _____ Christian counseling
24. _____ ministries to families

a. propagates the Gospel
b. volunteers
c. movements
d. numbers skyrocketing
e. social services
f. Media communications
g. service
h. missionary organizations, denominational staffs
i. for benefit of fellow believers
j. church related ministry
k. pastors and missionaries

1

Choose the correct answer (each answer, 2 points).

25. A career is ____ .

   a. a planned process   b. a vocational decision   c. a temporary choice

26. Concerning the career development pattern, the young adult enters a period of ____ .

   a. transition   b. anticipation   c. clarification

27. Church planting is often done by members of the ____ staff.

   a. pastoral   b. office   c. denominational

28. A youth director is often a member of the ____ staff.

   a. pastoral   b. office   c. denominational

29. Halfway houses seek to convert and to rehabilitate ____ .

   a. alcoholics   b. drug addicts   c. both a and b

30. Christian support services that construct buildings and maintain facilities are rendered by ____ .

   a. laborers   b. skilled workers   c. technicians

31. Photographers are ____ .

   a. laborers   b. skilled workers   c. technicians

32. *The Dictionary of Occupational Titles*, published by the United States Department of Labor, describes about ____ thousand occupations.

   a. ten   b. twenty–nine   c. forty

33. The *first* responsibility of a Christian school is to have ____ .

   a. an excellent academic program

   b. an economically efficient program

   c. personal models of good values

   d. a personalized learning system

34. All of the following statements describe a career *except* ____ .

   a. A career is more than a single vocational decision.

   b. A career is concerned with long–range planning.

   c. A career usually unfolds with a series of similar jobs.

   d. A career results from purposeful planning.

   e. A career is chosen to establish a way of living

Answer this question (this question, 5 points).

35. A Christian in secular work wisely witnesses by what three means?

   a. _____

   b. _____

   c. _____

NOTES

3

2.26   Rescue missions on skid row reach down–and–out ____ .
        a. transients   c. alcoholics
        b. married couples   d. a and c

2.27   Conference centers are popular with ____ , especially during the summertime.
        a. children   c. adults
        b. youth   d. all ages

2.28   Ministries to families are ____ .
        a. multiplying   c. diminishing
        b. remaining the same   d. nonexistent

SCHOOLS

The need for Christian teachers is growing as the number of Christian schools skyrocket. Elementary and secondary schools are spreading rapidly.

Christian teachers themselves especially need adequate education. The more advanced their teaching level, the more they usually specialize by concentrating on just one subject. Teacher's aides are either helpers or trainees, and other instructors are specialists in music, art, library resources, recreation, drama, or other subjects.

Preschool and Kindergarten personnel serve to help parents and care for younger children. Their greatest contribution is imparting Christian attitudes in and encouraging Christian relationships among the children. In order to reflect the character of God, Christian schools should exceed all other schools in academic excellence. Christian schools call for teachers who are models of Christian values, and integrate a Christian world-view (viewpoint) into every subject. The elementary teacher must be suited to the grade levels he (or she) teaches. Christian junior high and high schools usually provide a wider range of educational services than elementary schools do, including counseling and extra-curricular (nonrequired) activities such as music and athletics.

Christian college teachers are separated more exclusively into "religious" and "secular" departments. The teaching of Bible, doctrine, and theology subjects are obviously ministries in themselves; but the humanities, arts, and sciences also have their rightful place. Colleges employ a more diversified staff, including deans of students, resident "parents," Christian service supervisors, traveling representatives, and others.

Seminary professors, who are often ordained, excel in their special fields; Some teaching scholarly, doctrinal subjects, while others train students to perform smoothly in preaching, conducting church ceremonies, and so forth. In common with denominational staffs, seminary positions have an advanced entry level usually reserved for those who have been outstanding in their previous ministries.

Complete this activity.

2.29   Underline the following Christian school ministries that appeal to you. Then number those you have underlined in the order of their appeal to you, beginning with one for the most appealing.

____ teacher's aide   ____ school counselor
____ preschool teacher   ____ music teacher
____ elementary teacher   ____ librarian
____ high school teacher   ____ athletic coach
____ college religion teacher   ____ dean of students
____ college teacher (other)   ____ Christian service supervisor
____ seminary Bible teacher   ____ school representative
____ seminary performance teacher   ____ other: _____

Answer these questions.

2.30   Why is the need for Christian teachers growing? _____

_____

2.31   What do seminary positions have in common with denominational staffs? _____

_____

2.32   What quality of academic programs should Christian schools provide? _____

_____

2.33   What is the responsibility of individual teachers in a Christian school? _____

_____

2.34   How does the professional preparation of elementary teachers and high school teachers differ.

_____

SOCIAL SERVICES

Social services create unique inroads to persons with special needs. Many of these services have been standard ministries on foreign mission fields. Christian adoption agencies locate Christian homes for babies in the United States and abroad. Some Christians open their homes to foster children and youth who have been disowned or are wards of the court. Childcare centers initiate ministries with parents as well as youngsters.

Halfway houses seek to rehabilitate and proclaim the Gospel to alcoholics, drug addicts, and other delinquents. "Christian communes" are typically cultic (rather than true Christianity), but some have pointed converts from eccentric cultures in the right direction.

Christian counseling centers meet a number of needs: psychological, emotional, relational, social, and spiritual as they employ pastors, psychologists, psychiatrists, social workers, physicians, and other special counselors and consultants. Psychiatrists are doctors of both medicine and psychology. Social workers assist people in improving their living conditions, often making contacts for people to find homes, schools, and places of employment. Some Christian ministries serve the needs of the disabled: the mentally ill, the crippled, the blind, the deaf, and the sick. Nurses occasionally find employment with large Christian institutions. For example, many Christian rest homes and retirement villages minister to senior citizens.

Complete this activity.

2.35   Underline the following *social service ministries* that appeal to you. Then number those you have underlined in the order of their appeal to you, beginning with one for the most appealing.

____ adoption service   ____ counselor

____ foster home   ____ psychiatrist

____ child care   ____ social worker

____ drug rehabilitation   ____ medical worker

____ delinquent rehabilitation   ____ the mentally ill

____ street people   ____ the disabled

____ ghetto   ____ the mute

____ the deaf   ____ the blind

____ rest home   ____ other: _____

Complete these statements.

2.36   Some Christians open their homes to _____ who have been disowned or have become wards of the court.

2.37   Halfway houses seek to Christianize and rehabilitate a. _____ , b. _____ , and other c. _____ .

2.38   Psychiatrists are doctors of both a. _____ and b. _____ .

2.39   Christian homes for babies in the United States and from abroad are located by Christian _____ agencies.

2.40   Christian rest homes and retirement villages minister to _____ .

MEDIA COMMUNICATIONS

The media provides ample venues for communicating a Christian message. Christian journalism is a busy ministry, with editors, writers, and reporters being employed on a variety of bases. At least four hundred daily newspapers across the United States use religious news editors. Computer software production and the Internet are excellent tools. A steady stream of Christian literature flows from book publishers, periodical staffs, Sunday school lesson presses and church publications. One denomination alone publishes about one hundred fifty different periodicals. Numerous publications require designers and illustrators. Literature distributors, retailers, and librarians perform a ministry as they exercise discretion in recommending titles to their stock.

Christian broadcasting has fewer job openings but it is perhaps more influential. Writers, producers, and announcers are needed for Christian radio and television stations both at home and abroad. Such media utilize technical as well as artistic talents.

Complete this activity.

2.41   Underline the following media communications ministries that appeal to you. Then number those you have underlined in the order of their appeal to you, beginning with one for the most appealing.

____ publication editor   ____ broadcast writer

____ publication writer   ____ radio producer

____ publication reporter   ____ television producer

____ publisher   ____ radio announcer

____ newspaper religion editor   ____ television announcer

____ graphic designer or illustrator   ____ actor

____ bookstore manager   ____ software producer

____ literature salesman   ____ web site developer

____ other _____   ____ animation

Answer *true* **or** *false*.

2.42   _____   At least four hundred newspapers across the United States employ religious news editors.

2.43   _____   Christian journalism is a busy industry.

2.44   _____   Although *distribution is not a ministry*, distributors of Christian literature exercise spiritual discretion.

2.45   _____   Although Christian broadcasting usually has fewer job openings, it is an influential ministry.

SUPPORT SERVICES

This final category of Christian services underlies all other organized ministries. It represents occupations that are not usually performed as Christian ministries but that are essential to the operation of churches and Christian organizations. Many Christian lay people are not skilled in vocational ministries, but by performing basic services for Christian organizations, they are part of the Lord's work. These services include laborers, skilled workers, and technicians.

Laborers. Laborers construct buildings and maintain facilities for churches, Christian schools, and other Christian organizations at home and abroad, such as in church building departments. Some Christian corporations specialize in church buildings. A conscientious church custodian performs a valuable service in maintaining a beautiful building.

Skilled workers. Skilled workers of all sorts keep Christian organizations operating smoothly. An office staff is essential. Specialized ministries are performed by personnel managers, accountants, public relations agents, buyers, marketing specialists, printers, cooks, dietitians, and many others.

Technicians. Technicians are in demand increasingly by Christian ministries. Data processors and computer programmers are used by schools, research agencies, and large organizations. Electronic technicians service radio and television

LABORERS MAINTAIN FACILITIES.

stations in addition to public address and recording installations. Pilots and airplane mechanics keep missionaries and supplies flying over the mission field. Churches with fleets of buses need mechanics to service them. Photographers are a part of the graphic arts staffs. Architects and draftsmen occasionally develop church school buildings.

 Complete this activity.

2.46   Underline the following Christian support services that appeal to you. Then number those you have underlined in the order of their appeal to you, beginning with one for the most appealing.

___ carpenter		___ data processor
___ custodian		___ computer programmer
___ office clerk		___ electronics technician
___ personnel manager		___ pilot
___ accountant		___ mechanic
___ buyer		___ photographer
___ marketing specialist		___ architect
___ printer		___ draftsman
___ cook		___ public relations agent
___ dietitian		___ other: _____

Match these items by writing the correct letter on each line.

2.47 ____ accountant

2.48 ____ airplane mechanic

2.49 ____ draftsman

2.50 ____ printer

a. laborers

b. skilled workers

c. technicians

 In your *career notebook*, list in the order you have numbered them, all of the ministries that you have marked under these seven categories. Renumber them all in the order of their appeal to you, beginning with the number *one* for the most appealing. This is your master list of specific ministries in order of their priority for you (Assignment 11).

Review the material in this section in preparation for the Self Test. This Self Test will check your mastery of this particular section as well as your knowledge of the previous section.

Answer *true* or *false* (each answer, 1 point).

2.01 _____ Two classifications of New Testament ministries are general service and special ministries.

2.02 _____ General services in the New Testament are rendered primarily for the benefit of fellow believers.

2.03 _____ Special ministries are based on the New Testament but are duties performed principally in obedience to the church.

2.04 _____ *Ministry* in the New Testament is synonymous with *service*.

2.05 _____ The restrictive meaning of ministry identifies it as the Gospel ministry; pastors.

2.06 _____ The inclusive meaning of ministry identifies it as the volunteer ministry.

2.07 _____ To be a "minister," one must be ordained and "enter the ministry."

2.08 _____ A ministry need not be religious in nature.

2.09 _____ If one's occupation is not a ministry, he cannot have a ministry.

2.010 _____ Christian custodians can minister in a church by their work.

Complete these items (each answer, 3 points).

2.011 Pastors of smaller churches are likely to have _____ (more, fewer) functions than pastors of larger churches.

2.012 A church administrator manages the _____ and properties of the church.

2.013 Denominational staffs are usually chosen for a particular ministry because they _____ in that ministry.

2.014 According to a survey, the number of churches that serve two hundred people or less is _____ out of every five churches.

2.015 The principal difference between missions and other ministries is the _____ of service.

2.016 The category of Christian ministries that utilizes the most varied ministries is _____ .

2.017 Chaplaincy ministries are provided mainly for a. _____ , b. _____ , and c. _____ .

2.018 Any organized ministry in the United States that is not self–supporting can be categorized in a broad sense as _____ .

2.019 One Christian ministry that attempts to attract street people and to convert them to Christ is often conducted in _____ .

2.020 The most extensive programs among Christian movements during the past few decades minister to _____ .

2.021 Servicemen centers are located strategically to reach military personnel on _____ .

2.022 The number of _____ is skyrocketing.

2.023 Christian schools should provide a _____ standard of education than do secular schools.

Choose the correct answer (each answer, 2 points).

2.024   A director of Christian education is a member of the _____ staff.
        a. pastoral   b. office   c. denominational

2.025   The editor of a church publication is a member of the _____ staff.
        a. pastoral   b. office   c. denominational

2.026   A youth director is often a member of the _____ staff.
        a. pastoral   b. office   c. denominational

2.027   Church planting is often done by members of the _____ staff.
        a. pastoral   b. office   c. denominational

2.028   Ministries to families are _____ .
        a. nonexistent   b. multiplying   c. diminishing

2.029   Halfway houses seek to rehabilitate and give the gospel to _____ .
        a. alcoholics   b. drug addicts   c. both a and b

2.030   Christian support services that construct buildings and maintain facilities are rendered by
        _____ .
        a. laborers   b. skilled workers   c. technicians

2.031   When missionaries rely on pilots and airplane mechanics, they are relying on _____ .
        a. laborers   b. skilled workers   c. technicians

2.032   Photographers are _____ .
        a. laborers   b. skilled workers   c. technicians

2.033   A church custodian is a _____ .
        a. laborer   b. skilled worker   c. technician

Answer these questions (each answer, 5 points).

2.034   What is the New Testament meaning of *ministry*? _____
_____
_____

2.035   What is the first responsibility of individual teachers in a Christian school? _____
_____

2.036   What do seminary positions have in common with denominational staffs? _____
_____
_____

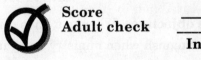

Score _____
Adult check _____
                                  Initial   Date

III. MINISTRY VS. CAREER

Anita Webster and Rachel Keller graduated from high school together. The two girls were drawn to one another because they were both dedicated Christians. Their friendship blossomed during their senior year. After ten years they are still dedicated to the Lord, but their careers have led them in different directions. Anita became a missionary to Africa, whereas Rachel was married soon after graduation. A Christian housewife and mother, Rachel serves actively in her church. She was instrumental in her friends conversions and growth in Christ.

Mark Benson and Shawn Robbins were high school buddies also. Now Mark is Shawn's pastor. Their church is new and small; therefore, Mark works at a part time job. Shawn serves as an officer of the church. His Christian character has a strong influence in the grocery store that he manages.

Which of these four people is performing a ministry? The missionary and the pastor receive unanimous votes; their ministries are their careers. The housewife and the businessman are not in *vocational* ministries; but, they too serve in ministries apart from their vocations.

A ministry and a career may either be the same, or separate. Anita and Mark are serving the Lord in vocational ministries. Rachel and Shawn are serving the Lord just as acceptably in volunteer ministries.

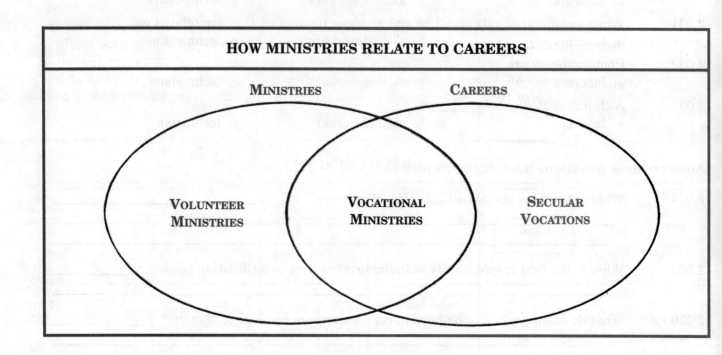

HOW MINISTRIES RELATE TO CAREERS

MINISTRIES   CAREERS

VOLUNTEER MINISTRIES   VOCATIONAL MINISTRIES   SECULAR VOCATIONS

SECTION OBJECTIVES

Review these objectives. When you have completed this section, you should be able to:

1. Distinguish when ministry and career are the same.
2. Distinguish when ministry and career are separate.

VOCABULARY

Study these words to enhance your learning success in this section.

career	occupation
job	vocation

WHEN THEY ARE THE SAME

Career. The definition of a career is frequently misunderstood. A career is more than a single vocational decision, such as for immediate employment. Rather, career concerns the long-range projection and more than a vocation. A vocation simply unfolds into a series of similar **jobs**, but a career results from purposeful planning. One takes up an **occupation** primarily to *earn* a living, but one chooses his career to establish a *way* of living.

A career can be defined as a *planned process of vocational development.* This planning includes necessary preparation and training to develop required skills for a career is a process projected through one's entire lifetime. A Christian's career is approached in much the same manner as a ministry. Of both, the question is asked, "What is my mission in life?"

Career development. Career development follows a pattern. Vocational specialists describe career phases as follows: An adolescent is in a period of anticipation where they begin clarifying their commitment to the working world. The young adult is in a period of transition, which passes through schooling, training, apprenticeship, and vocational placement.

Career ministries. Career ministries vary from full to part time participation, and in recent years, mission boards have appealed for short term service. A summer term on the mission field is great for prospective missionary candidates who wish to "try out" for missions, a one to five year term gives retired people an opportunity to serve for a limited time and a short term may be used as a second vocation or be sandwiched in as a volunteer ministry. While others use a short term as a leave of absence from a regular job. In any case short term service corresponds to the Biblical call to a single temporary mission, similar to that of Gideon (Judges 6).

Churches and Christian organizations that are limited financially profit from part time staffs as this method produces a larger and more diversified ministering staff. This gives those not in vocational ministries the opportunity to participate on a part-time basis.

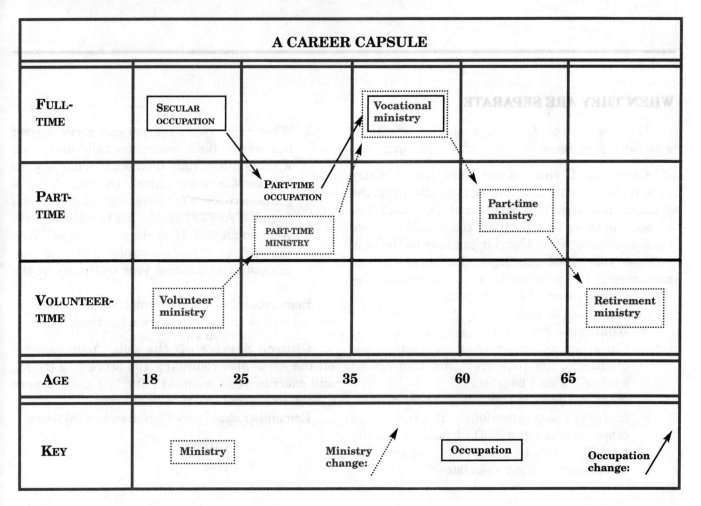

A CAREER CAPSULE

✐ Complete these statements.

3.1 One may have a vocational ministry, or he may have a volunteer a. _____ with a secular b. _____ .

3.2 A single vocational decision usually concerns _____ employment.

3.3 A career concerns a _____ projection.

3.4 A career includes more than a single _____ .

3.5 One takes up a/an _____ primarily to earn a living.

3.6 A series of similar jobs may be considered one's _____ .

3.7 One chooses his _____ to establish a way of living.

3.8 A planned process of vocational development is one's _____ .

3.9 A process that is projected throughout one's lifetime is his _____

3.10 Concerning both his career and his ministry, a Christian asks, " _____
_____ ?"

✐ Answer true or false.

3.11 _____ Concerning the development of a career, an adolescent is in a period of transition.

3.12 _____ Relative to the career–development pattern, the young adult is in a period of anticipation.

3.13 _____ The degrees of career ministries vary from part–time to full–time participation.

3.14 _____ "Full–time Christian service" is just one level of vocational ministry.

3.15 _____ Short–term service is particularly helpful in small churches.

WHEN THEY ARE SEPARATE

Do I serve the Lord in a secular vocation? Absolutely, you serve Him on and off the job.

Christian Living on the Job. Your ministry in a secular occupation differs radically from the primary ministry, but be assured that God has placed you there for a purpose. You should be more than a "Sunday" Christian, for you may be the only believer your associates know. You serve God by ministering to their needs as the opportunities arise by three means: by what you are, by what you do, and by what you say.

1. What you *are* on the job reveals your Christian *character*. Ask yourself these questions: "Am I sincere?" "Am I an honest worker?" "Can I be trusted?"

2. What you *do* on the job refers to your *actions*. Answer these questions: "Do I make a conscientious effort?" "Do I produce quality work?" "Do I genuinely regard the achievements of my associates?"

3. What you *say* on the job can carry a good *testimony*. Both your shoptalk and your witness affect your testimony. What is your motive for witnessing? Do you have a genuine concern for your associates? Are you friendly? Are you careful not to rob time from your employer? How do you witness? Your answers to these questions will help you evaluate and improve your testimony on the job.

Remember that not all ministries are vocations, but all well-done vocations are ministries.

Church Service off the Job. Your ministry off the job is also voluntary. You serve in a church and exercise your spiritual gifts. You grow in your Christian life and live it in your home.

Remember that *every* Christian is a minister.

Answer these questions.

3.16 A Christian in secular work wisely witnesses by which three means?

a. _____

b. _____

c. _____

3.17 In what three principal environments can a Christian have "volunteer" ministries?

a. _____

b. _____

c. _____

3.18 What are three questions one should ask himself relative to his character on the job?

a. _____

b. _____

c. _____

3.19 What are three questions one should ask himself relative to his actions at work?

a. _____

b. _____

c. _____

3.20 Should one take time out from his work to witness? _____

_____

Before you take this last Self Test, you may want to do one or more of these self checks.

1. _____ Read the objectives. Determine if you can do them.

2. _____ Restudy the material related to any objectives that you cannot do.

3. _____ Use the SQ3R study procedure to review the material:
   a. **Scan** the sections.
   b. **Question** yourself again (review the questions you wrote initially).
   c. **Read** to answer your questions.
   d. **Recite** the answers to yourself.
   e. **Review** areas you didn't understand.

4. _____ Review all activities and Self Tests, writing a correct answer for each wrong answer.

Match these items (each answer, 2 points).

3.01	_____ ministry	a. volunteers
3.02	_____ director of Christian education	b. propagate the Gospel
3.03	_____ general service	c. in the United States, not self-supporting
3.04	_____ foreign missions	d. pastors, missionaries only
3.05	_____ special ministry	e. church planter
3.06	_____ church publication editor	f. skilled worker
3.07	_____ restrictive meaning	g. office staff
3.08	_____ home missionary	h. for benefit of fellow believers
3.09	_____ inclusive meaning	i. most varied ministries
3.010	_____ home missions	j. pastoral staff
		k. service

Answer _true_ or _false_ (each answer, 1 point).

3.011 _____ Every Christian should have a career ministry.

3.012 _____ A Christian can have a ministry in a secular occupation.

3.013 _____ A career is a planned process of vocational development.

3.014 _____ A series of similar jobs may be considered a vocation.

3.015 _____ Christians do not serve God in secular occupations.

3.016 _____ One takes up an occupation to establish a way of living.

3.017 _____ All ministries are not vocations, but all well-done vocations are ministries.

3.018 _____ One should take time from his secular work to witness.

3.019 _____ Every Christian is a minister.

3.020 _____ One's ministry off the job is served voluntarily.

Choose the correct answer (each answer, 2 points).

3.021 In the New Testament, the term _ministry_ refers mainly to _____ .

    a. deacons   c. volunteer service

    b. religious activity

3.022 A Christian with a secular occupation can have a ministry _____ .

    a. on the job   c. both a and b

    b. off the job

3.023 A career is _____ .

    a. a planned process   c. a one-time choice

    b. a vocational decision

3.024 Relative to the career-development pattern, the adolescent is in a period of _____ .

    a. transition   c. preparation

    b. anticipation

3.025 Concerning the career-development pattern, the young adult enters a period of _____ .

    a. transition   c. clarification

    b. anticipation

3.026   A Christian in secular work witnesses wisely by _____ .

       a. What they are: their character   d. a and c

       b. What they do: their actions   e. a, b and c

       c. What they say: their testimony

3.027   A Christian can have a "volunteer" ministry _____ .

       a. at work   d. a and b

       b. at church   e. a, b and c

       c. in the home

3.028   Onesimus _____ .

       a. ministered to the church at Antioch   d. a and c

       b. rendered Paul personal aid   e. a, b and c

       c. ministered to the church at Philemon

3.029   The *first* responsibility of a Christian school is to have _____ .

       a. an excellent academic program   c. personal models of good values

       b. an economically efficient program   d. a personalized learning system

3.030   All of the following statements describe a career *except* _____ .

       a. A career is more than a single vocational decision.

       b. A career is concerned with long-range projection.

       c. A career usually unfolds in a series of similar jobs.

       d. A career results from purposeful planning.

       e. A career is chosen to establish a way of living.

Answer these questions in complete sentences (each question, 5 points).

3.031   What is the meaning of this statement: "A ministry need not be sacred in nature"?

       _____

       _____

       _____

3.032   What quality of academic programs should Christian schools provide? _____

       _____

3.033   What three questions should one ask himself relative to his character on the job?

       a. _____

       b. _____

       c. _____

3.034   What three questions should one ask himself relative to his actions at work?

       a. _____

       b. _____

       c. _____

Score _____

Adult check _____

                           Initial   Date

Before you take the LIFEPAC Test, you may want to do one or more of these self checks.

1. ____ Read the objectives. Determine if you can do them.
2. ____ Restudy the material related to any objectives that you cannot do.
3. ____ Use the SQ3R study procedure to review the material.
4. ____ Review all activities and Self Tests, and LIFEPAC Glossary.
5. ____ Restudy areas of weakness indicated by the last Self Test.

GLOSSARY

career. A planned process of vocational development; a general course of action or progress through life.

job. A piece of work, often for a fixed period of time.

occupation. One's business, employment, or trade; work one does regularly or to earn his living.

vocation. An occupational calling; an occupation, business, profession or trade.